URICH SCHOOL

CASS CO. R-VIII ELEMENTARY SCHOOLS
GARDEN CITY URICH, MISSOURI

Science-Hobby Book of
Bird Watching

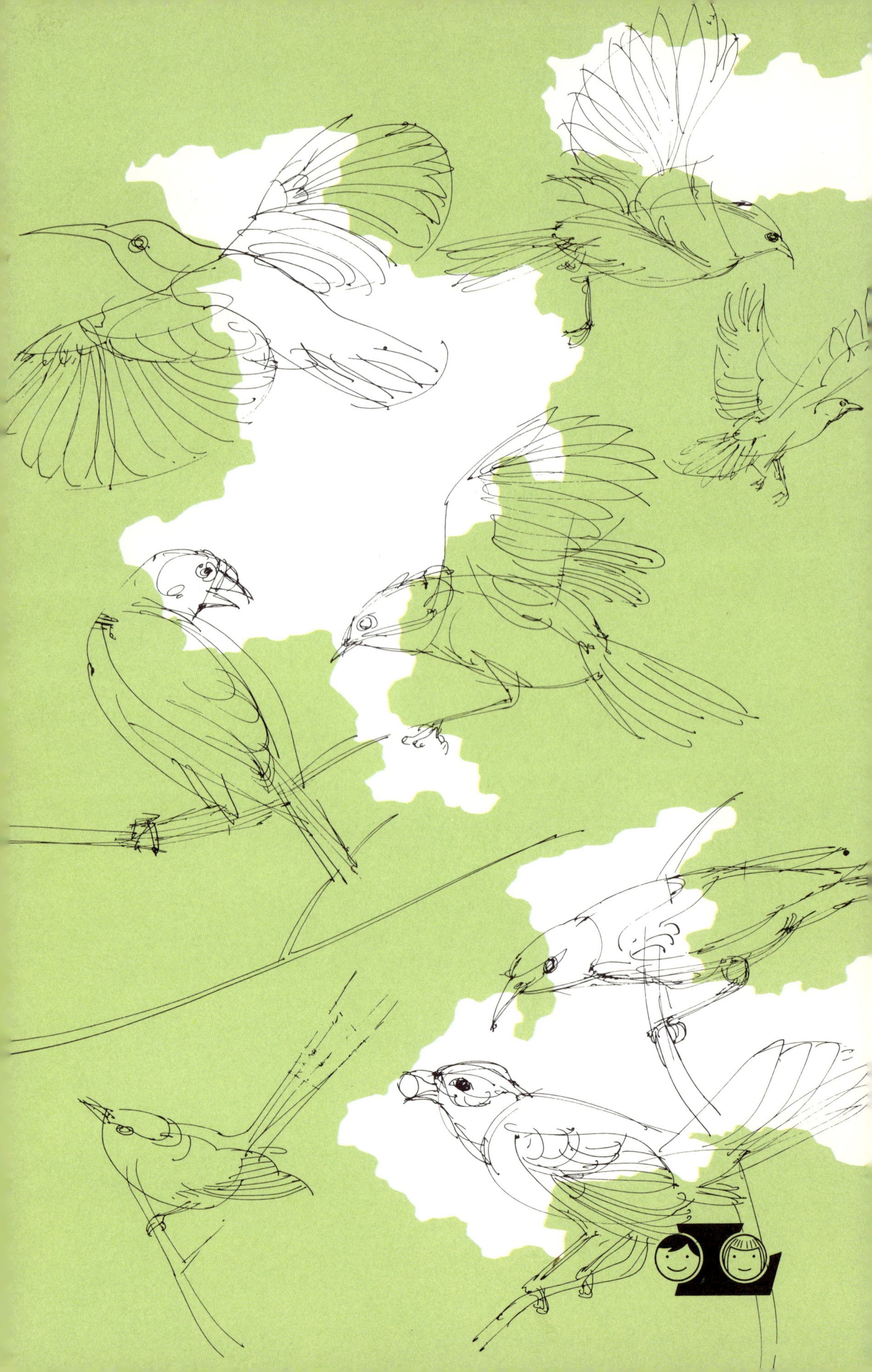

Science-Hobby Book of
Bird Watching

by
ROBERT WELLS

FOREWORD BY
Roland C. Clement
Staff Biologist
NATIONAL AUDUBON SOCIETY

Published by
LERNER PUBLICATIONS COMPANY
Minneapolis, Minnesota

to
Nancy Detrick

Second Printing 1971

Revised edition copyright © 1968 by Lerner Publications Company
Original copyright © MCMLXII by Hammond Incorporated

International Standard Book Number: 0-8225-0553-3
Library of Congress Catalog Card Number: 68-54182

Manufactured in the United States of America
All rights reserved

Foreword

Next to other humans, birds are by far the most interesting of our neighbors. They are such an interestingly diversified group!

Fortunately, also, they are more and more widely appreciated. Perhaps this is because birds sing and dance so much that their lives seem happier and less clouded than our more complicated lives. Birds solve life's problems by instinct; we have to think out ours. As a result, we not only admire birds when we come to know them but, I suspect, most of us envy them.

In any event, there is no doubt that birds can enrich our lives. Getting to know them is part of our need to feel at home on this planet.

Few of us live on farms next to the soil. So we need a contact with the ageless realities of Nature. Bird watching is such a contact, and it has already provided an ideal tie to Nature for millions of people in our generation. As Mr. Wells has emphasized in this attractive book, bird watching has the commendable trait of being elastic: you can take it in small doses or "ride your hobby" until you graduate into professional ranks, as have many of us.

The legion of bird watchers, already estimated to number some ten million Americans, is sure to increase, and books like this one will help pave the way.

Have fun!

ROLAND C. CLEMENT
Staff Biologist
NATIONAL AUDUBON SOCIETY

CONTENTS

Why Bird Watch 7
How to Bird Watch 8
    Structural Characteristics 9
When and Where to Look 10
Activities 11
Local Bird Watching 12
Recognition of Birds 13
    Field Guides 13
    Habitat 16
    Ornithology Books 16
Backyard Bird Watching 16
    Feeding 16
    Species Commonly Found 18
    Feeding Techniques 19
    Houses, Feeders, Baths 21
    Plantings 22
Birdhouse Dimensions 25
Photographing Birds 26
Bird Walks 27
    Binocular Selection 28
    Activities That May Be Observed 29
Migration 30
    Map of 6 Main Flyways 31
Territory Establishment 32
Courtship 32
Nest Building 34
Incubation 35
Plumage 37
Calls and Songs 37
Field Trips 38
Record Keeping 40
    Bird Clubs 44
    Feeding 44
    Plantings 45
    Wildlife Leaflet 45

ROBIN
Turdus migratorius migratorius

Bird Watching as a Hobby

WHY BIRD WATCH

Bird watching means, to some people, bird identifying. There is a challenge in being quick enough to spot a fast-moving bird, recognizing its color, outline or kind of flight and then knowing — not guessing, but *knowing* — which of the many species of North American birds *this one* is.

To others, bird watching means not only recognizing birds but also observing what they are doing; and to still others, it means discovering *why* they are doing it. In any case there is as much to see as you want to see. The birds themselves are ideal for this purpose. Birds' lives are lived rapidly with a great deal of intensity. The feeding, migrating, raising of young, and all other life activities are compressed so that the activities encompassing an entire life cycle can be seen almost completely in only weeks. Compared with earthbound, plodding, silent humans, birds live with so much activity, color, and song that their lives appear concentrated — so vital is each activity.

Bird watching as a hobby can return to you as much as you can or wish to give it in time, interest, money, or energy. Like a good companion, it will respond to your wishes and provide you with pleasant times. It's fun — satisfying, rewarding, endless fun. *You* choose how much or little of it you want: whether to watch these brilliantly colored, quick creatures so different from all the world's others; whether to recognize many of them well enough to identify them when you encounter them; whether to observe these vital creatures — perhaps on a field trip to some area other than close to home

— and to understand the "what" and "why" of whatever you see; or, finally, whether to discover a piece of information about these creatures which thus far is unknown — to furnish scientific information of value.

The purpose of this book is to give information about bird-watching activities, which you may choose, and tell you how to proceed. If you find later that your interest has deepened, then this book will furnish you more information, or tell you where and how to find it. But that is only if you want it: this is *your* hobby.

HOW TO BIRD WATCH

To enjoy it most, you should teach yourself to observe. Not just to look, but to look closely. *Observe*. Really *see*. This is rewarding, for you will discover things you have never noticed. Not only are these birds small or large, of bright or dull plumage, but also they are of a variety of shapes and sizes; some walk, some run, some hop, some waddle; some perch in trees, others in bushes; some perch high, some low; the flight of some is on a straight line, others dip. Why? And what are they eating? If all birds don't eat the same kind of foods, what does each type eat? You may be feeding some one day to lure them closer to you.

RING-BILLED GULL
Larus delawarensis

HUMMINGBIRD
Family Trochilidae

STRUCTURAL CHARACTERISTICS

To all creatures, food is of prime importance; certainly it is for birds. They need it to maintain the fast tempo of their lives which helps them escape their enemies who would eat them — that's probably why they learned to fly, long ago. This fast tempo calls for and results from a physiology of high body heat, fast heartbeat, rich red blood, and a rapid rate of converting food to body heat and energy. All this takes place in a body surprisingly fragile. The bones are hollow, the feathers, also. The lean muscular body under these feathers is surprisingly small — all part of the weight-saving design for flight. A very great part of the creature's strength is generated as well as consumed by the powerful breastbone muscle which makes the bird's wings beat. This muscle accounts for as much as half the total body weight of some birds.

Watch birds in flight, especially if they fly just over you. See the four or five separate primary feathers sticking out at the end of each wing, unless these birds are gulls. It is largely the action of these feathers, as the wing beats up and down, which propels the bird forward in flight. Watch the bird come in for a landing with the slot at the leading edge of the wing opened, like an airplane's, to smooth out the airflow over the wing and so maintain lift, even though speed is reduced to the stalling point.

There is even more of a challenge to those who would try to observe such quick intense creatures. They, fragile and defenseless, are equipped with other life-preserving devices: alertness, keen sight, brains, and wits. These, combined with the bird's small size, the camouflage of its covering in both color and pattern, and its quick movements, make it necessary for the bird watcher to discover how to approach closely enough to observe these creatures without frightening them away.

A danger signal to them is any quick movement in their direction. You must walk *slowly* as you approach. If you are watching the bird closely enough, you may be able to see whether it is aware of you and is showing signs of flying off. If it does stop, wait a while, and *then* slowly move closer. Do this quietly with occasional pauses if necessary. Take a zigzag course of approach, rather than a straight-line one. This gives the bird less cause for alarm and flight. But binoculars or a camera dangling by a strap from your shoulder may frighten the bird just by their swinging, as could your arms. Insure against this and against any shiny object from which the sun's rays might reflect, warning the bird of your approach.

It is an achievement to be able to approach one of these alert wild creatures. After enough practice, you may find that you are able to do some stalking: approach a bird without his being fully aware of you. Keep the sun at your back, if possible, for not only does this make it more difficult for the bird to see you; it also makes it easier for you to observe the bird, which is your objective. At this angle, sunlight will reflect the bird's true colors. The same bird seen at a different angle and in a different light might look quite drab. Again, move slowly and quietly, pause frequently for as long as it seems necessary. You'll discover that a bird, whose plumage well camouflages him, may let you approach fairly close before flying off. But an ill-camouflaged bird seems to know he must be more wary and may fly away much sooner.

WHEN AND WHERE TO LOOK

The time of day and type of terrain also may make a difference in your success. In early morning or late afternoon, the bird probably will be feeding, breaking its fast from the long night, or nourishing itself sufficiently for the long night to come. In the warmer months of the year or in the southern climates, to which some birds migrate, this need for food to maintain the bird's high body heat of some 106° F. is not as desperate as it is during bitter cold when insects have disappeared and berries, if any remain, are covered with ice. Then, during the dark night, this fragile creature's life may be measured only in hours. A few species are able to save themselves by becoming torpid — lowering body heat to extend the precious limited fuel supply within, for a day or two longer when food might once again become available.

Just which of the species of bird you are able to observe depends not only upon the season but also largely upon the section of the country. In addition, some birds may be year-round residents while others are migrants "passing through"; and still others are there only for the season — summer, or winter for the birds from still farther north. There are, of course, still

COMMON MALLARD
Anas platyrhynchos platyrhynchos

other reasons why "these" birds are "here"; "here" may be a woods, an unlikely place to look for ducks; or a pond where woodpeckers would find little business to transact; or a marsh, a meadow, or a sandspit at the seashore, each with the kinds of birds which prefer it.

Long ago, birds chose these types of dwelling areas and, as time passed, became more and more adapted to living there. The duck's webbed feet that paddle, the woodpecker's ability to cling to a tree trunk while feeding from it, the high-soaring hawk whose sharp eyes see its prey scurrying through the grass far below (then its steep, swift, pouncing dive), the differences between species and sub-species, all give bird watching a variety that makes its interest unlimited and unending.

This could make for endless confusion for the beginning bird watcher except that, in the life activities of birds, their patterns of behavior are quite similar, no matter what the species. The differences between species show most in the way in which each carries out these life activities.

ACTIVITIES

What are the life-cycle activities? For many, migration and then the establishment of territories at the new location by the males who fiercely guard these against others of their species. Their assertions of property rights usually are accompanied by song, an advertisement not only of ownership but also to the female, whose later migration brings her here to established territories and her future home. Courtship follows in a great variety of ways, often with great beauty of display and ceremony. Nesting, egg laying, and incubation follow, then the responsibilities of parenthood: raising the family well enough to migrate from winter's harshness, if these are migratory birds, in time and with enough strength to make the long trip.

LOCAL BIRD WATCHING

You can observe some of these activities while walking through areas within your own locale; even better, while in your own garden or backyard, if you choose to make it inviting to birds. You can begin bird watching right here, close to home. Even for city apartment dwellers there are parks, and in many of these there are a large variety of birds as free and as wild as those in the woods. Here is ample opportunity to accept the challenges offered by bird watching and to live, if only for an hour or two, among these uninhibited, graceful creatures.

This may be the point where you choose to stop and go no further into the hobby of bird watching for the present. Certainly the choice is yours. You know something of what bird watching can be. Now, you are observing where before you were only glancing carelessly; you perceive where formerly you did not even notice. You know enough about the construction of the birds to understand why they are quick, intense, fragile, and hungry. You know how to approach in order to observe them, and you know that there is a full cycle of life's activities to be witnessed, which is compressed not only into the brief time span of a bird's life but even into a few weeks. This is so intense as to be unmistakable. You can expect to find different kinds of birds in different kinds of areas. These will vary between sections of the country and between seasons of the year. If you go no farther than this, you are much richer than when you started.

BIRD FOUNTAIN

PERMANENT FOOD HOUSE

RECOGNITION OF BIRDS

FIELD GUIDES

This richness can grow, if you wish to study two types of books. One of these, called a "field guide," describes, by text and pictures, the characteristics by which you can recognize birds. Since there are more than six hundred species of birds — in North America alone, these field guides usually are limited to sections of the country: Eastern United States, Western United States, etc. Your librarian or your bookstore proprietor can show you these. And, of course, your local chapter of the National Audubon Society is quite willing to help you in your selection.

At the beginning of bird watching, your list should consist chiefly of the birds in your locale. Learn to recognize, first, those in your neighborhood. Eventually, you will be able to recognize dozens of species quickly and accurately. But the journey of a thousand miles begins with the first step. Study that local list. Then, when you decide you are ready for more, obtain the guides, lists, books, or color plates which describe the birds you can expect to find in your region or state.

Learning these lists is not all the fun. You should be out *looking* for birds, or watching for them through your window. The more you see of them, the more you become familiar with identifying features, such as shapes, colors, markings, and outlines in flight. Each species shares these, as well as other means of recognition. Perhaps it is a telltale characteristic such as the robin's cocking its head while "listening for a worm." Perhaps it is a unique and easily seen marking like the junco's white tail feathers that flash when he flies off. Perhaps it is a recognized song, like the jeering call of the blue jay.

It won't be long before you can spot and recognize these clues of identification; then you are well on your way. This is a short cut to recognition that *could* be memorized but need not be at this early stage. Later, if you are interested enough, you may learn all you can about each of these birds you now recognize so easily. So much the better if you do, for the more you learn about these creatures, the more you will enjoy this hobby. Of course, these single giveaway characteristics are not the only ways to identify the bird. There are also the clues of how it flies, how it walks, how it stands or perches, as well as the characteristics of size, color, song, and shape. The bird's habitat is also an important clue. The bird clinging to that tree trunk surely is no meadowlark: it is a woodpecker which gets its food from trees.

One caution about size. Books list these measurements as made from tip of tail to tip of beak of *dead* birds. Stretched out limply, the bird measures *longer* than he appears to be while alive. A little sparrow, for example, measures and is listed as *six* inches.

You may be pleasantly surprised to recall how many birds you already know and can identify. List them in your mind, now: sparrow, robin, duck, swan, eagle, turkey, hawk, stork, parrot, owl — build the list as long as you can.

ENGLISH SPARROW
Passer domesticus domesticus

SONG SPARROW
Melospiza melodia melodia

RED-WINGED BLACKBIRD
Agelaius phoeniceus phoeniceus

BALD EAGLE
Haliaeetus leucocephalus leucocephalus

BALTIMORE ORIOLE
Icterus galbula

EASTERN CROW
Corvus brachyrhynchos brachyrhynchos

RED-TAILED HAWK
Buteo borealis borealis

MOCKINGBIRD
Mimuspolyglottos polyglottos

HABITAT

An important clue to recognizing a bird is the *location* from which you are observing him. Birds can be grouped in several ways. One of these is by habitat. Those found near large bodies of water are gulls and the gull-like gannet, petrel, and shearwater, among others. Waterfowl, found close to water, are the duck, the goose, and the others resembling these in shape, such as the loon and the swan. Marshland birds have, for the most part, long legs and long bills: the crane, the heron, and the ibis are among these. The eagle, hawk, and owl are birds of prey. You usually will find the nuthatch and the woodpecker in trees, and the wren in bushes. Here too are the oriole, the tanager, and the chickadee. On the ground generally are the very familiar birds: the sparrow, crow, jay, starling, mockingbird, blackbird, lark, pigeon, and the birds that resemble the chicken such as the grouse and quail.

The field guide helps you in finding and then identifying these birds. It supplies the bird's picture, tells where it usually is found, describes the plumage, call, and principal characteristics. This is the first of the two types of books you will find helpful.

ORNITHOLOGY BOOKS

The second type of book is not primarily a guide, yet it will aid you in learning to identify birds. It tells what birds *are* and what the species share in common. It describes the "what," and "why," and "how" (so far as these are known) of migration and reproduction including courtship and nesting, and the anatomy of the bird itself. This is the kind of information which adds to your pleasure of bird watching, whether you choose bird identifying or progress to bird observing.

BACKYARD BIRD WATCHING

Your own garden or backyard should be good for both identifying and studying the activities of birds in your locale. You may wish to lure more birds there for these purposes. This can be accomplished by providing such essentials as food, water, shelter, and protection. But as you know, different species of birds differ in eating habits and in the shelter they need. Before buying bird feed or building birdhouses, discover *what kinds* these should be.

Even before you think of these things, think of this: birds are not toys; they are living creatures. They are fragile. Their lives depend, almost on a day-to-day basis, upon food which you now are considering providing for them. As living creatures, they respond to you giving them food which gives them life.

FEEDING

If for some reason this food is withheld, the bird's life may be in jeopardy. This is because most birds of the North migrate to the South long before winter, lest the scarcity of food make it impossible for them to maintain the high body heat necessary for their intense lives. If by feeding them you encourage them to remain beyond the time they would have begun their migration, they will not migrate. They must then remain through the winter almost entirely dependent upon you for the food, water, and shelter which mean life to them. This certainly is true for waterfowl; when their lake or marsh becomes icebound, they are practically helpless except for you. Unless you will provide these necessities daily, *without fail,* or unless you break off feeding well before migration time, don't begin to feed them at all. Your local Audubon Society chapter can tell you "when" for *your* locale.

You must feed them through the winter or cut off feeding in time for them to prepare *themselves* for migration by foraging for their food during the last few weeks before migration time. This will add interest and pleasure to your hobby.

What to feed them? Learn first the birds in your locale from the local chapter of the Audubon Society, state guide, or perhaps from a field guide if it is that specific. Maybe you have already seen and identified the various species in your area. The U.S. Department of Agriculture publishes a table

FEEDING STATION   COCONUT LARDER

of winter foods eaten by those birds you are most likely to attract. But here again you should use your own imagination. Offer a variety of these foods to your birds and learn *which* are the ones they will eat, before you buy or prepare foods in quantity. Use a feeding tray divided into compartments made of cardboard strips, or other material. Fill these with different types of foods — and soon you will know which *your* birds prefer. Mix into the grain some ground oyster or clam shells, or coarse white sand. This grit, hard for the birds to obtain in winter, substitutes for teeth in grinding food, not in their mouths but in their gizzards.

Feeding in summer usually presents no problem to the birds; nature is generous then. If you wish to supplement what nature is providing, you might again experiment with your feeding tray, this time trying fruits, ground peanuts, and crumbs of bread or cake. They may also like cereals, such as rice, oats, or wheat. And don't forget their supply of drinking water.

SPECIES COMMONLY FOUND

Among the birds you attract, you probably will find the robin, Baltimore oriole, bluebird, catbird, wren, and most of the songbirds we know. These birds spend the summer in the North and then fly to the South in the early fall for the winter. Some of the thrushes and sparrows winter in the South, too, but spend the summers farther north. A very few others nest quite far north and come south to the middle latitudes for the winter; the winter wren, the junco, and the tree sparrow are some of these. Then, of course, in middle latitudes there are such year-round residents as the English sparrow, starling, crow, blue jay, chickadee, cardinal, nuthatch, woodpecker, and many others. Like some of the summer residents, who remain to be fed, these too will enjoy your bounty and will reward you with their presence.

CARDINAL
Richmondena cardinalis cardinalis

NORTHERN BLUE JAY
Cyanocitta cristata cristata

FEEDING TECHNIQUES

How to do this feeding: Obtain some suet (birds prefer white rather than yellow) from your butcher. Hammer a nail through a piece of it into the bark of a tree, sufficiently high to let the bird feel reasonably safe from cats. Here on the tree's bark, too, is the place to smear peanut butter. If you find that the larger birds are tearing loose and carrying off large chunks of this suet, try tying the suet to a limb of the tree. Use plenty of soft cotton cord and wind it tightly around the suet. If the suet still is being worked loose and carried off in large amounts, drill one-inch holes in a short length of log (one-and-one-half feet), pack these well with suet, and hang the log from a tree limb.

As for the seed, scatter it on the ground. If deep snow interferes with the birds' getting it, place the seed on a large cloth. Fasten down the edges so that the cloth will not be blown over by the wind. *After* you find that the seeds you've scattered have attracted a crop of birds, you may wish to install feeder devices. These are usually of wood and specially designed for this purpose.

WHITE-BREASTED NUTHATCH
Sitta carolinensis carolinensis

STARLING
Sturnus vulgaris vulgaris

FOOD HOPPER

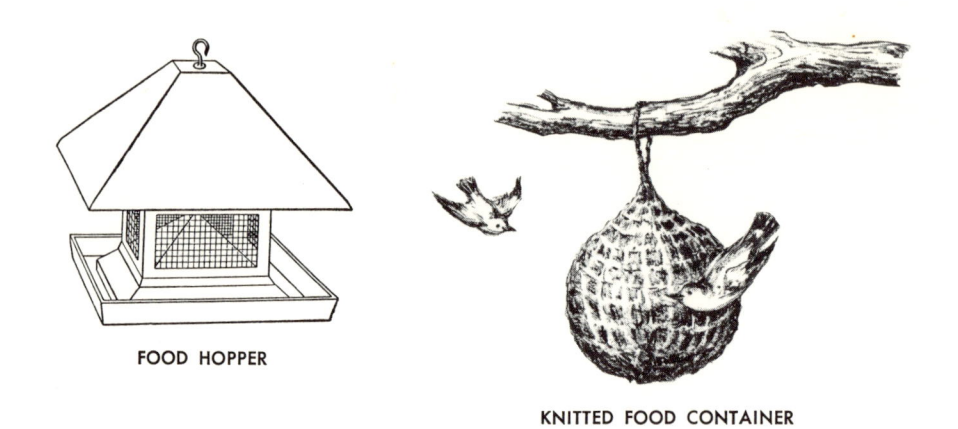

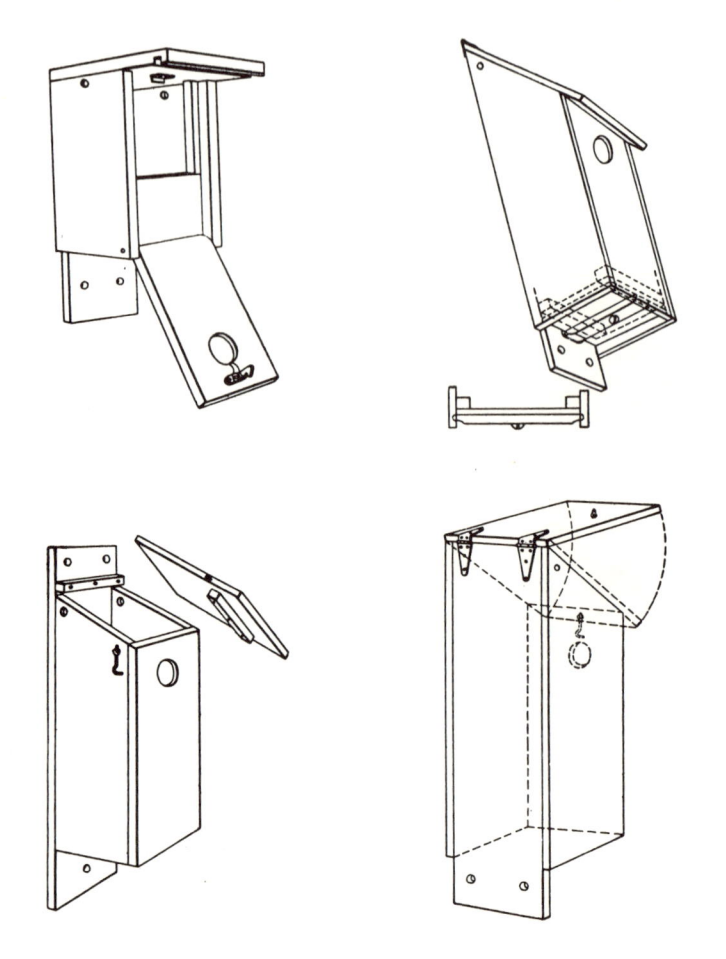

KNITTED FOOD CONTAINER

VARIOUS TYPES OF BIRDHOUSES

HOUSES, FEEDERS, BATHS

You may wish to install birdhouses or bird shelters, which are one-side-open houses, facing downwind. Birdbaths, if well designed and placed, will attract passing birds — sometimes, one rarely seen in your part of the country. This is important to note and report.

These items can be purchased or you can build your own. Whether you build or buy, decide first just what is really *needed* and then produce it, not to suit your taste but what you know would be the bird's taste. Do it with a bird's-eye view, as it were. For example, feeders, houses, and shelters should generally be of wood, have surfaces rough enough for the bird's feet to grip, and look natural. For a birdhouse, the entrance should be round, like a hole going into a hollowed nesting spot in a tree, *not* an un-birdlike square. An exception, though, is the horizontal slot which the wren prefers.

As with the food, different kinds of birds require different types of birdhouses. The dimensions for these differ slightly, not much but enough to make it wise to discover first just which of these you will need before buying or building. You'll find, too, that you don't need as many as you believed at first. Of course, the *kind* of bird you attract and the type of backyard you have will decide the quantity; one birdhouse — or maybe two — is usually the limit for a half acre. Where should these be placed? Place in trees fastened to the trunk or hung from a branch whose height is to the liking of *that* species. However, atop poles is a popular location, too. But these houses should have some shade as do the tree-located houses, lest the fledgling birds inside suffer from too much heat.

If the feeding tray is placed close to the window, it will provide a source of interest and pleasure. If it is possible to select the window on the basis of what is best for the bird, so much the better. These considerations are safety and comfort. The bird should have a bush or thicket close by to reach quickly in case of danger. For the bird's comfort, the winter feeding tray might be located where it is out of the wind and, if possible, in the warm sunshine. Safety and comfort should determine the location also of feeders atop poles.

Birdbaths certainly should be located near bushes to provide safety, preferably in more than one direction. The bird with *wet* feathers is already handicapped in its dash away from sudden attack. Sunlight is needed here, too, with a place to perch where the bird may dry his feathers. Shade also is needed in the birdbath's location. If, to the *sight* of water, there can be added the *sound* of dripping or running water, even more birds will be attracted. A birdbath may be no more than a shallow pan of water set on a slight slope of ground. The slope makes both shallow and deeper water, for the small and the large birds which come to drink as well as to bathe. You may want to build or buy a more elaborate birdbath. Remember that birds prefer something which is familiar to them: the water on the ground (although they don't seem to mind birdbaths being on stands) and a shallow and rough-surfaced place, such as the edge of a pond or brook.

CASS CO. R-VIII ELEMENTARY SCHOOLS
GARDEN CITY URICH, MISSOURI

PLANTINGS

Decide if you wish to plant vines, bushes, or trees which will attract, protect, and feed birds. Your experience may tell you which these will be, or you may write to the U.S. Fish and Wildlife Service, Washington, D.C. for lists of shrubs and trees, as well as a list of the various birds which like each kind best. Of course, the Audubon Society can help here, too. The size of your backyard and the section of the country, in which it is located, will determine your choice from the wide selection available.

Food is scare in winter. In your plantings, make certain there is a good source of food among the fruits and berries which remain through the winter. This is vital for the birds. Since many kinds of birds live on berries and fruits, these plantings can supply a great deal of food for a surprisingly large number of these creatures who need daily nourishment during late winter and early spring.

The limbs of the trees and shrubs can be cut and shaped so that, as they grow, they will form crotches where birds will like to build nests. Vines grown over these will form a shelter which birds like for the protection it gives to them and their nests. This kind of protection is furnished for some birds by the needles of pine, fir, and spruce trees. Protection against storms and winds, also, is given to the birds by the dense foliage of these trees thickets, and vines.

If you find that your hobby justifies planting *many* of these shrubs and trees, then you will want to plan carefully before you start to buy and to work. Don't forget *your* own enjoyment. Select those plantings whose flowers, colors, heights, and shapes will best suit your yard and your neighborhood. How far apart to space these and just where should be determined by the size and characteristics of these plantings. For the birds' part, they seem to prefer open spaces between clumps of vegetation, rather than solid, dense vegetation. Perhaps most important, though, is the food these plantings supply to the birds. Consider during which months each plant produces its food so that several will provide a continuous food supply. Should there be variety in the foods, so much the better.

WESTERN TANAGER
P. ludoviciana

RUBY-THROATED HUMMINGBIRD
Archilochus colubris

ROSE-BREASTED GROSBEAK
Pheucticus ludovicianus

SCARLET TANAGER
Piranga erythromelas

SOME OF OUR COLORFUL BIRDS

MARTIN HOUSE

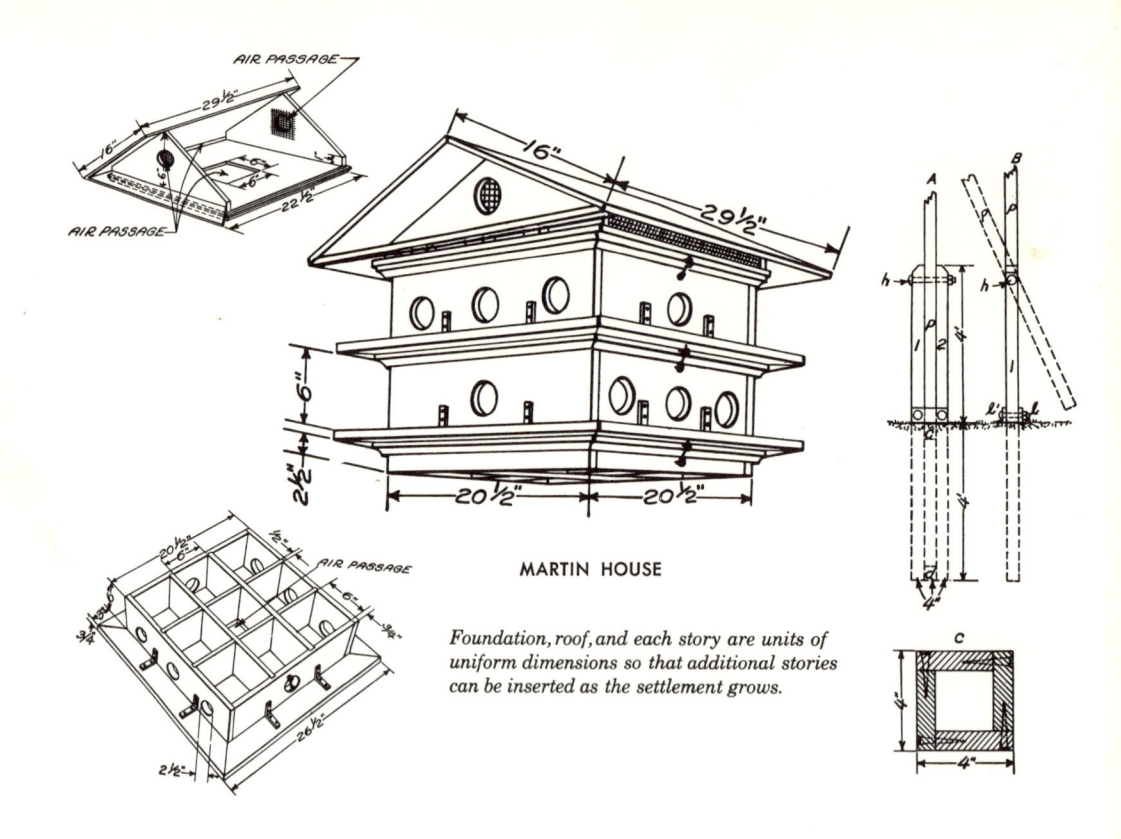

Foundation, roof, and each story are units of uniform dimensions so that additional stories can be inserted as the settlement grows.

NEST BRACKETS AND SHELVES

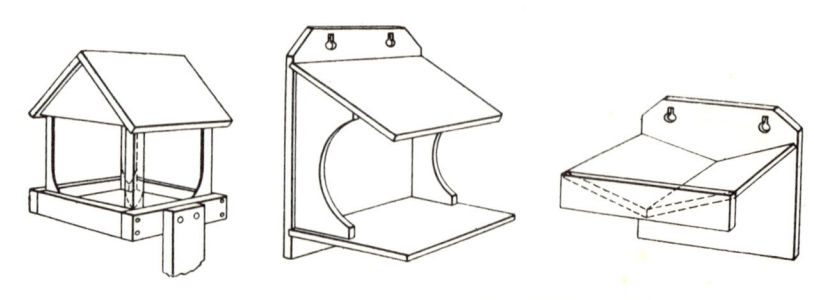

NESTING SHELVES DIMENSIONS
Open sides (see illustration)

BIRD	FLOOR (INCHES)	DEPTH OF BOX (INCHES)	HEIGHT ABOVE GROUND (FEET)
Robin	6 x 8	8	6 - 15
Barn swallow	6 x 6	6	8 - 12
Phoebe	6 x 6	6	8 - 12
Song sparrow	6 x 6	6	1 - 3

(Information taken from Conservation Bulletin #14)

BIRDHOUSE DIMENSIONS

BIRD	FLOOR (INCHES)	DEPTH OF CAVITY (INCHES)	ENTRANCE HEIGHT FROM FLOOR (INCHES)	DIAMETER OF ENTRANCE (INCHES)	HEIGHT FROM GROUND (FEET)
Bluebird	5 x 5	8	6	1½	5 - 10
Chickadee	4 x 4	8 - 10	6 - 8	1⅛	6 - 15
Titmouse	4 x 4	8 - 10	6 - 8	1¼	6 - 15
Nuthatch	4 x 4	8 - 10	6 - 8	1¼	12 - 20
House wren, Bewick's wren	4 x 4	6 - 8	4 - 6	1 - 1¼	6 - 10
Carolina wren	4 x 4	6 - 8	4 - 6	1½	6 - 10
Violet-green and Tree swallow	5 x 5	6	1 - 5	1½	10 - 15
Purple martin	(see illustrations)				
House finch	6 x 6	6	4	2	8 - 12
Starling	6 x 6	16 - 18	14 - 16	2	10 - 25
Crested flycatcher	6 x 6	8 - 10	6 - 8	2	8 - 20
Flicker	7 x 7	16 - 18	14 - 16	2½	6 - 20
Golden-fronted woodpecker, Red-headed woodpecker	6 x 6	12 - 15	9 - 12	2	12 - 20
Downy woodpecker	4 x 4	8 - 10	6 - 8	1¼	6 - 20
Hairy woodpecker	6 x 6	12 - 15	9 - 12	1½	12 - 20
Screech owl	8 x 8	12 - 15	9 - 12	3	10 - 30
Saw-whet owl	6 x 6	10 - 12	8 - 10	2½	12 - 20
Barn owl	10 x 18	15 - 18	4	6	12 - 18
Sparrow hawk	8 x 8	12 - 15	9 - 12	3	10 - 30
Wood duck	10 x 18	10 - 24	12 - 16	4	10 - 20

(Information taken from "Homes for Birds," U.S. Department of the Interior, Fish & Wildlife Service, Washington, D.C. 20025; Conservation Bulletin #14 for sale by the Superintendent of Documents, U.S. Government Printing Office, Washington, D.C. 20025.)

PHOTOGRAPHING BIRDS

If you plant wisely and well, and if the birds are attracted, you should be able to enjoy still another aspect of your hobby: photographing the birds. Here, with their own natural setting forming the best kind of background, these brilliantly colored creatures are beautiful subjects for pictures. These pictures are all the more interesting when they show the bird in one of its many activities: bathing in your birdbath, feeding in your berry bushes, or — at still closer range, through the window — at your window-feeding shelf, or quietly brooding in the nest.

Of course, you must be both photographer and ornithologist to be able to take really fine pictures. But even the experts once were amateurs. Start the easy way. Take pictures of the birds which are more bold than shy. These won't fly away before you can get close enough, especially if your movements are unhurried and quiet when you approach. Don't let your equipment — even its cords or straps — flap, or blow in the breeze. Chickadees are one of the birds which are less timid; they are common enough for you to find almost anywhere, and they usually are near at hand throughout the year. These friendly little birds frequently can be coaxed to eat out of your hand — a highly prized picture if your assistant photographer is quick enough.

Be careful in photographing birds at a nest of fledglings. If you frighten the parents very badly, they may fly away and not return at all. This, of course, is fatal for the fledglings. But this should not happen if you are reasonable in what you are doing. Quite naturally, the bird, which is incubating its eggs or brooding its young, doesn't want strangers approaching the nest. The longer the bird has been at these activities, the more reluctant it is to leave the eggs or baby birds. It must be especially difficult, then, for this defenseless creature to remain in the face of what looks so dangerous — a shiny-lensed camera pointed at close range by an enormous human. Again, be reasonable in what you are doing; make sure you are not frightening the bird too much; take your picture quickly and go quietly.

True, the birds may fly away from nest, bath, perch, or feeder but they are such creatures of habit, you can expect them to return. If you have gone to considerable trouble to get your camera in position or to build some sort of blind, you will probably wait for the bird to return again. This interim time is good for readying your camera or other equipment so that you are entirely prepared to "shoot" when the bird reappears.

Decide the kind of camera and film to get and whether or not to use flash bulbs. Let your camera dealer help you. If you already have a camera, then your question is the choice of film, perhaps color, for the kind of picture you desire.

Always try to improve on each group of pictures you take — either in technique, selection of film, or composition of the picture itself. Certainly you will do this before spending considerable money on camera equipment.

If your camera has a tripod, you may wish to aim the camera at a chosen spot and then move away to operate it by remote control. Make sure the tripod's legs are secured so that the camera won't be pulled over when operated. This is particularly apt to occur if you pull the shutter release by a long string. A smooth fishing line can be used. Avoid tangling it in the shrubbery. Later, if you find that you're good at photographing birds, you may want to look for electrically operated shutter-tripping devices for remote control. Prices of movie cameras are now considerably less expensive and their film, too, is comparatively less expensive than previously. Here is a whole new area of "hunting by camera" to keep in mind if your interest in this hobby deepens.

BIRD WALKS

On your walks, your camera, movie or still, will serve you well. Of course, you will need to have had some experience in using your equipment by the time you take it on walks, for it is more difficult to obtain good pictures under these conditions than working with familiar areas and backgrounds, such as your own backyard.

BLACK-CAPPED CHICKADEE
Parus atricapillus atricapillus

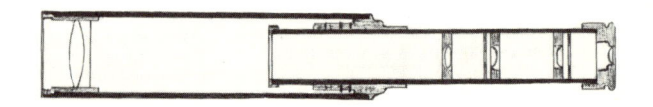

TELESCOPE

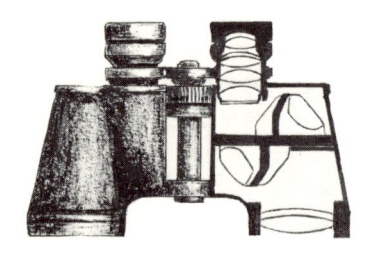

BINOCULARS

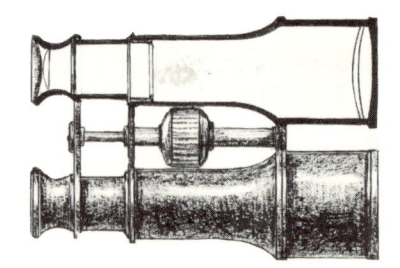

FIELD GLASSES

BINOCULAR SELECTION

Binoculars, too, are excellent for use on walks and even in backyard observing. Since good ones can be quite expensive, it is wise not to buy any until you know you will really use them. New binoculars can cost as much as $200 or more; however, good secondhand ones will serve quite well.

There's another good reason for waiting until you have enjoyed this hobby for a while before buying expensive binoculars. They are made in a variety of models, each with specific characteristics. Some are fine for watching birds at the shore — for a long distance; others are better for closer use while on walks; still others, less powerful, would be the best choice if most of your bird watching is done in your own backyard.

A reliable dealer will help you in your selection. He probably will talk in terms of the binocular's power, relative brightness, and field of view, and of coated lenses, individual or center focus, as well as durability and weight. These are simple terms. "Power" is magnification: how much bigger does the bird appear to be than it really is? "Seven power" or "7x" means, of course, seven times as large or seven times closer to you than the distance it now is. Considering that a two-power glass (as most opera glasses are) would show you twice as much as you now see, a seven-power glass — most common among really earnest bird watchers — is truly powerful.

Relative brightness, as the name suggests, refers to the light-gathering capability of the glasses and, therefore, how brightly and distinctly they represent the bird to your eyes. Lenses which are coated make brighter images because the coating reduces the amount of light the lenses otherwise would reflect and thus lose.

The ability of the glasses to be focused quickly is important for you. Not only does the individual bird cover distances quickly, but the watcher's attention may be drawn suddenly from one bird which is near, to another farther away. For this reason, center focus, which adjusts *both* lenses simul-

BINOCULAR MAGNIFICATION

6 Times   7 Times   8 Times   9 Times

As seen by the naked eye

taneously, seems generally more popular among bird watchers. Focus of individual eye pieces takes longer, of course, but it does make precision focusing possible.

Field of view is another consideration in which experience will guide you. It means how many feet *wide,* 1,000 yards away, you will see through the binoculars. Although the wider field permits you to pick out and hold moving objects easier, this feature may be at the cost of less power in certain glasses. Price, too, may be another factor.

Durability is important. Glasses knocked out of alignment because of careless handling are expensive to repair. This is especially true if they are very cheap and poorly designed, for these may not remain long in alignment. As for weight, this depends upon your own muscle power. In all, choose your binoculars by what suits *you* best and only after you know you will use them enough to enjoy them. Certainly they will help you to see very much more than your unaided eye could perceive.

ACTIVITIES THAT MAY BE OBSERVED

There is a great deal to see, for you are recognizing which one of the many activities in their life cycle these birds are doing. Moreover, you know *why* they are doing this; why this species nests here and not there; why that large stranger in the nest is being fed by a parent not its own (possibly of a species even *smaller* than the baby bird); the "why," in fact, of many life activities of these vital, quick, beautiful, different creatures.

The books which have given answers to these "whys" oddly enough cannot yet answer some other "whys" because those answers are not yet known. Perhaps it may be that after long and careful observation, after keeping accurate records of these observations, after learning what is now known of that particular activity, *you* may be the one to contribute information which would begin to explain "why."

MIGRATION

Migration of birds is one of these questions not yet fully answered. Why and how is this accomplished? How does the bird know that it must fly away from "here" and that "now" is the time? How does it know where to go? How does it navigate there, unerringly, year after year? And then, these same questions asked again for the return trip. So finely developed is this instrument or this mechanism that birds — their legs banded earlier for identity — have been known to migrate back, not only to the area of their summer quarters, but even to the neighborhood and the backyard whose feeding tray and birdbath they apparently remember having enjoyed the previous year.

In banding, the bird is caught in a way that neither harms nor frightens it, and a tiny lightweight metal band is affixed loosely to its leg. On the band are instructions to write to the Fish and Wildlife Service in Washington, D.C., U.S.A. Then the bird is set free. Banding is done mostly at feeding stations by bird fanciers who have been granted a permit by the government to do this work.

The distances of migration often are great. Although the robin and the bluebird travel only to the southern part of the United States for the winter, the wood thrush continues on to Central America, and the veery, as far as the northern part of South America; and the golden plover flies until it reaches Argentina. Certainly these destinations are far beyond the places where food and milder climate may be found. The eastern golden plover, which summers in North Siberia, spends its winters in the Pacific islands, flying by way of the Aleutian Islands and Hawaii. These are land birds, and each of these over-water hops is more than 2,000 miles. Why does one bird go there, and others go different distances and places? Why should the Arctic tern, a small seabird, feel it must fly each year from the Arctic to the Antarctic and back again, a round-trip distance of some 20,000 miles?

Perhaps a clue is in the behavior of caged birds. When it is migrating time for their species, they act restlessly in their cages. Obviously, they want to travel with their fellows. That restless feeling and that impulse to migrate must come then from within them, since they already have food and warmth in their cages.

As you watch the birds returning to their nesting areas, to the same birdbath, feeding their own young or those of other birds in the same way — each species in its own way — it becomes even clearer that it is such impulses which control so much of the life activities of the bird. These urges coming from within just must be obeyed. Moreover, these impulses instinctively seem to follow a set timing; and one impulse succeeds another. Migration home is followed by other sets of impulses; an early one is courtship.

In most species, migration by the males precedes that of the females. The earliest arrivals are those species which wintered close by — the robins, for example, which begin to appear from our South in March. Toward the latter half of April, you will see the arrival of the spotted sandpiper and the swallow. Those which have wintered in Central and South America appear in May; the warbler and vireos are among these. With the arrival of the shorebirds in early June, migration ends.

SIX MAIN FLYWAYS

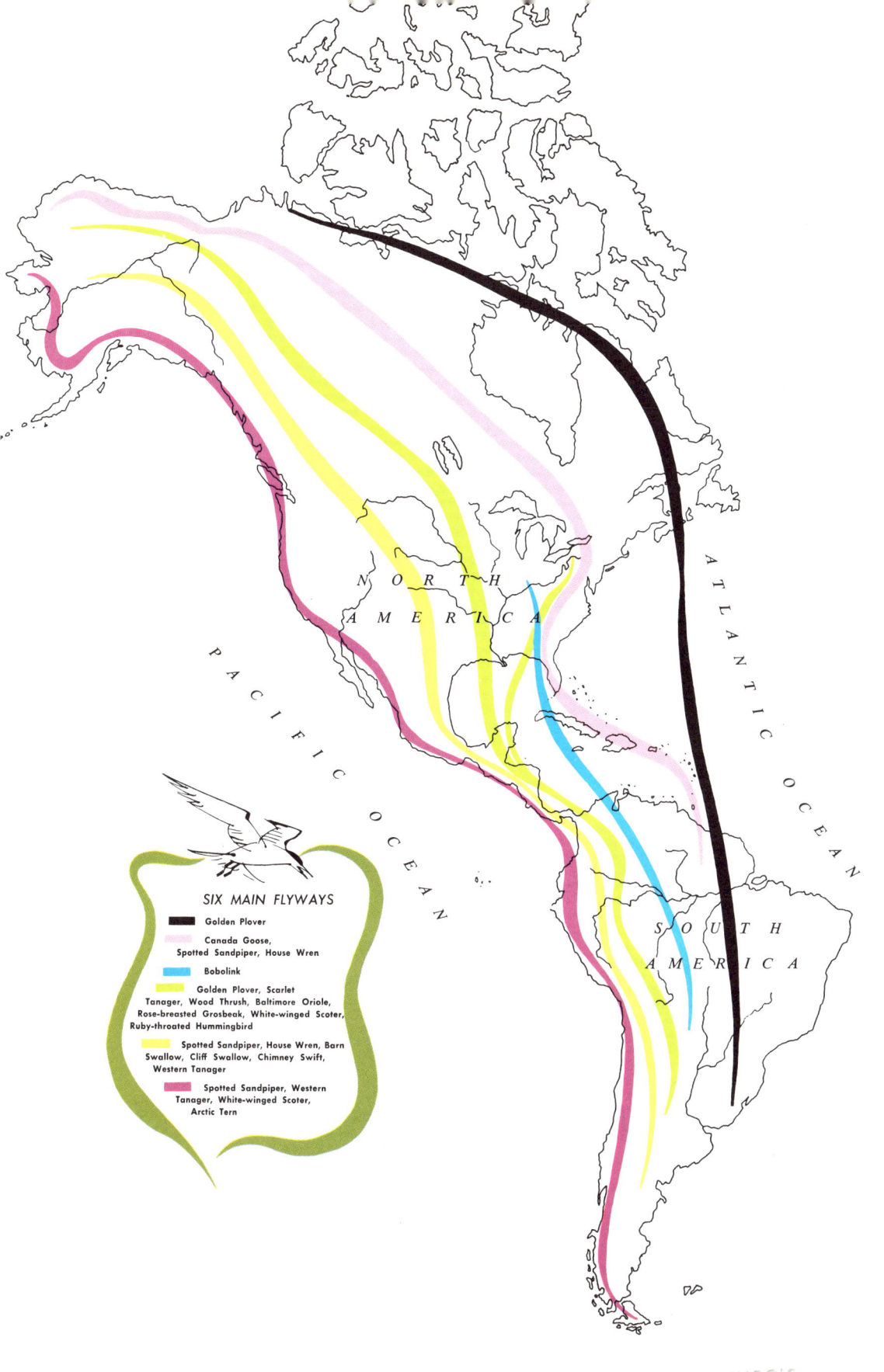

- Golden Plover
- Canada Goose, Spotted Sandpiper, House Wren
- Bobolink
- Golden Plover, Scarlet Tanager, Wood Thrush, Baltimore Oriole, Rose-breasted Grosbeak, White-winged Scoter, Ruby-throated Hummingbird
- Spotted Sandpiper, House Wren, Barn Swallow, Cliff Swallow, Chimney Swift, Western Tanager
- Spotted Sandpiper, Western Tanager, White-winged Scoter, Arctic Tern

CASS CO. R-VIII ELEMENTARY SCHOOLS
GARDEN CITY URICH, MISSOURI

One day, the birds are not here; the next day, they have arrived.

This is because most birds migrate at night. Of course, the darkness furnishes more protection; also most birds cannot feed as they fly (the swallows are an exception). They must see and be able to find their food not just on the open ground but in the denser kinds of vegetation, too. In their migration, these birds, sparrows and warblers among them, are obliged sometimes to fly over large areas where no food at all is available. By flying all night, they arrive in the morning when they can begin promptly their search for food. But if they flew all day, a night-arrival time would make them wait — perhaps an extra twelve hours, hungry after their exertion — until daylight and the opportunity to search for food.

This timing of flights also brings them another benefit: a nighttime takeoff has permitted them to feed all day — to "fuel up," as it were. It is this "fueling up" which also keeps the birds feeding, for perhaps two or three days at their stops en route. Not all birds fly the 2,000-mile hops of the golden plover!

TERRITORY ESTABLISHMENT

When the males arrive to take up residence, each promptly "stakes a claim" to a territory. This is an area large enough to provide food for him, for the mate he will attract from among the females migrating here later and for their future offspring. The size of this clearly defined territory varies with the species and the area. For example, a robin is about 250 yards from his neighboring robin; skylarks are about 350 yards from each other; but birds feeding on insects from trees settle within 100 yards or so of each other. Nor do insect eaters compete with seedeaters for a territory; it will support them both.

But it probably won't support two families of the *same* species. And so the male staking his claim to this territory must defend it. This means fighting and contesting, sometimes for weeks. If he is a first arrival, he can be expected to select the choicest territory, and if he is an older bird he probably will drive away a younger challenger. Often birds are observed fighting their reflections in windows or even in such shiny objects as auto hubcaps. When you observe this, you will know that here is a male who sees an interloper and is trying to fight him away from his territory.

You also will hear loud songs from these males. These are aggressive announcements of ownership rights. Song is answered by a similar song from a neighbor, back and forth, so that territories finally become not only established but also recognized. This actually saves considerable bickering among the birds later on about boundaries.

COURTSHIP

The song means something else, too. It tells a female of the species, when she has migrated later to the area, that here may be her mate, with an established territory and its supply of food, which will be kept safe by the male during the nesting period to follow. If she is attracted, the male may court her, usually by displaying his plumage. The peacock's special plumes on its tail comprise, perhaps, the most beautiful of all bird displays. Other birds, too, display their feathers to best advantage. Like the peacock, they court by dancing or running in front of the female.

Although the birds of the pheasant family may display the most impressive plumage of all, other and less handsome birds court by additional means. Some bring presents of food; others "show off" by stunt flying; still others dance, wave their wings or walk, seemingly proudly, before the female. All have their special ways of courtship. The bird watcher who has become adept can observe and discover a great amount of interesting detail in this courtship behavior of even our everyday birds. These details, if properly observed, will form a *pattern* of behavior and it is a pattern which the inquiring bird watcher seeks.

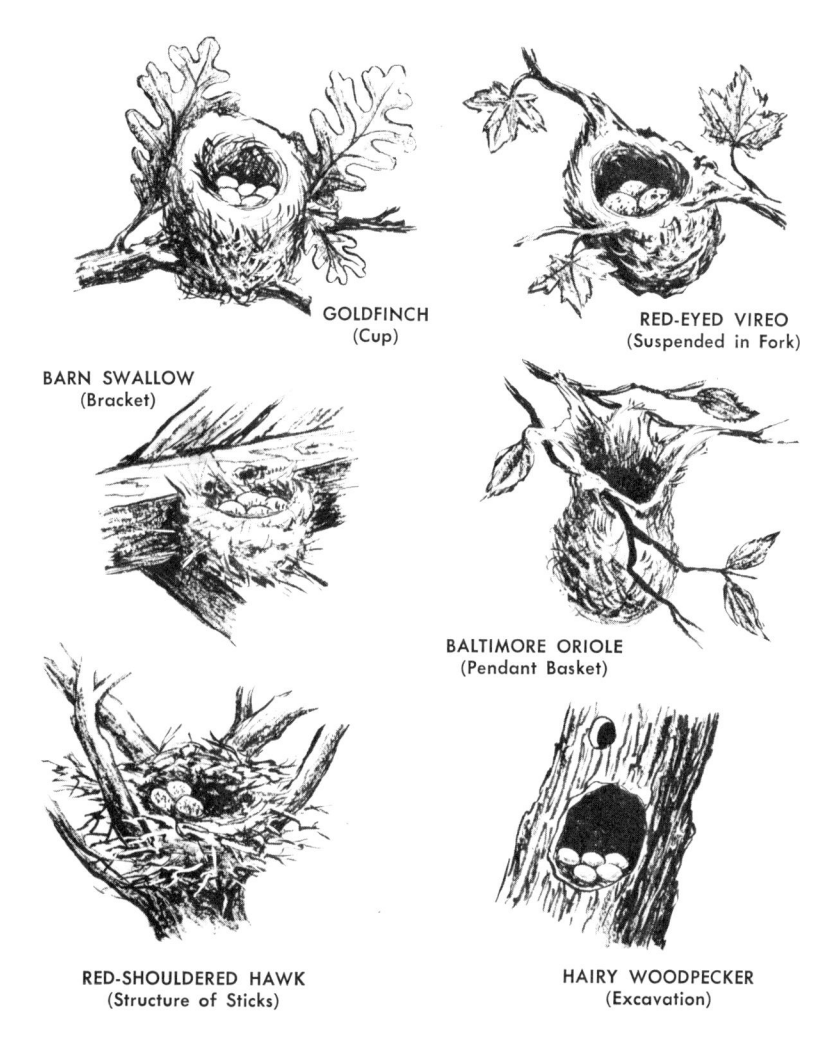

GOLDFINCH
(Cup)

RED-EYED VIREO
(Suspended in Fork)

BARN SWALLOW
(Bracket)

BALTIMORE ORIOLE
(Pendant Basket)

RED-SHOULDERED HAWK
(Structure of Sticks)

HAIRY WOODPECKER
(Excavation)

VARIOUS TYPES OF BIRDS' NESTS

MUTE SWAN
Cygnus olor

NEST BUILDING

When the male's courtship has been successful and the female has accepted him and the territory he offers her, they begin their nest building. Again, this differs among the species in which one of the pair builds the nest, if it is not a joint effort. Certainly the size, location, and construction of the nest are different among many of the species. If you see only one bird doing the nest building, it probably is the female. If the nest is of grass, it may belong to a bluebird; if of twigs, to a house wren; if of milkweed, to a Baltimore oriole. As you might expect, the stuff of which the nest is made is the grass, twigs, dead leaves, or marsh grasses of the area in which the bird lives.

These materials are used not only because they are available, but because when made into nests, most of them become almost a part of the landscape — another of nature's camouflage tricks for protection. To this trick the birds add another, concealment. And it is not only in the foliage of trees but also behind the cover of shrubbery and among the long grasses that these nests are built. Some are built even in burrows into the side of a sandbank. Since, as you know, birds live in woods, fields, or marshes, their nests are there in all these kinds of nesting sites. Yet you may not notice any nests at all, so well are they concealed. If you find one of the young on the ground where it has been lost out of its nest, let the parents find it by its cries for food. Do no more — at most — than to put it out of reach of cats, if you don't know where its nest is.

Some bird watchers enjoy a separate hobby, that is the art of finding and identifying birds' nests. There are so many kinds and so many different kinds of eggs, that identifying nests can very well be a hobby by itself. Some bird watchers even *collect* last year's nests. One should be very careful, however, never to disturb a nest which might yet be inhabited. It is necessary to obtain both a U.S. and a state collecting permit for this.

INCUBATION

The use of the nest is to provide a safe place for the eggs and their incubation and to prepare the fledglings for their lives in the outside world. Here again it usually is the female's job to keep the eggs warm with her body. The male may occasionally relieve her, especially if his plumage is not much brighter than hers and so does not attract unwanted visitors.

INDIAN PEAFOWL
Pavo cristatus

If incubation were to begin with the laying of the first egg and continue as each egg was laid each day — or each two days, in the case of the larger birds — then the first-laid egg would be the first-hatched egg. The first-hatched fledgling would have a head start over his brothers and sisters — to their disadvantage, when feeding time came. So, except for a few species, incubation starts when all the eggs are laid. It varies in length of time among the different kinds of birds: 12 or 13 days for sparrows, 13 or 14 for thrushes, 21 to 30 for ducks, etc. At the end of that period, the young peck their way out of their shells and begin life in the open world of their nest.

Some, when hatched, are covered with down, others are naked. The former are said to be precocial; the latter, altricial. These latter include jays, waxwings, flickers and most songbirds. The former include ducks, swans, geese and grouse. (These water birds need the insulation and buoyancy of feathers, early.) There also are in-between groups. Some precocial young soon start searching for their own food, but you will have the opportunity to observe most of the other kind in your area being fed by their parents.

Here again you will observe a variety of feeding methods. In the chief one, however, the parent inserts its bill with food deep into the gaping mouth and throat of the young. Others, the mourning dove among them, feed by regurgitation; or others feed by letting the young remove the food from inside the bills or throats of the parents, as do the jays and the herons. Your own observations of this feeding process will give you a wealth of information.

There are too many methods of feeding practiced by birds, distributed over areas far wider than you will use for your hobby, to attempt to list here. But you may do more than just watch — although that in itself is fun. If you observe and note carefully the details of what you make the effort to see, you will discover the *pattern* of behavior of *that* kind of bird in this process of feeding its young: note the astonishingly large amount of food required by each youngster. How many trips does the parent bird make to bring food? Is it only the male, or does the female go searching for food, too? How much time is there between trips, and how long do the trips take? When the parent bird returns to the nest, is it always from the same direction,

RUSTIC BIRDHOUSES

or is the bird wary, approaching the nest from a different direction each time? Answers to these and still more questions will tell you not only about the bird's feeding behavior but even more about the bird itself. That should open new vistas, for this information will evoke different questions; answers to these will yield still more information about this bird and possibly about birds generally.

PLUMAGE

Here in the nest, the young grow and acquire something of a plumage, the juvenal, which is replaced later by their adult plumage. In fact, most adult birds change their coats, too. They replace their old feathers, but in a sequence that does not leave them helpless. After the breeding season they molt, shedding their bright plumage for the more drab colors which blend better with winter's bare landscape. By the next spring, these feathers will have become sufficiently worn to need replacing and the bird will grow the brightly colored coat for courtship. The experienced bird watcher knows not only the bright coat but also the winter coat; moreover, he can tell the differences between those of the male, the female, and the young bloods.

Some birds never have brilliant plumage, for example, certain sparrows, while the chickadee, on the other hand, has an equally bright coat for the male, the female, and the immature — and in *all* seasons. In some species, only the males are brilliantly plumed; but of these, some are brilliant all year, others only during the breeding season.

CALLS AND SONGS

In the nest, the young also learn the calls for food and for help. It appears that these, unlike the songs of each species, are understood and acted upon by almost all birds. Songs are sung by adult birds, usually the males. Since this singing is used so much for establishing a territory and for attracting a mate, the bird apparently wants to make his whereabouts known for both these purposes. It finds a place to perch while singing where it can be seen easily. This is a great aid to you in your hobby. Your attention will be guided to the bird by the direction of its song. The song will tell you the kind of bird for which you will be looking. With that information you'll know whether to look high in the trees if it's a song sparrow you hear, or to the top of a fence post if it's a meadowlark. In early fall, though, these birds' songs are gone, along with their brilliant plumage. Instead of living separately, they draw together into flocks; instead of singing, they feed — not just in the mornings and late afternoons but most of the day. This extends your bird watching time. All of these activities mean that the birds are preparing for migration.

How do you learn which of the many species of birds is singing *this* song? It isn't easy, but when you do learn, you have still another means by which to enjoy this hobby. There are books which illustrate, by a kind of shorthand and with explanations, the individual songs of a great many birds. There also are recordings of bird songs. Your librarian can help you, too, in selecting books and phonograph records; so can the local chapter of the birdwatching society.

MOURNING DOVE
Zenaidura macroura carolinensis

WOODTHRUSH
Hylocichla mustelina

FIELD TRIPS

You now are well along in this hobby of bird watching if you are able to observe not only with your eyes but also with your ears. You are ready now to go farther afield — Bird Finding Guides can specify the areas — or to take a cross-country hike. An old hand at this hobby would refer to that merely as a "bird walk." More than likely, this veteran bird watcher can suggest the route for you.

Probably this route will not take you deep into the woods for most birds prefer trees and bushes where there is more sunlight than penetrates a forest. However, among the exceptions are the wood thrush and the blue jay. Look higher in the trees for the warbler and the oriole; and look lower for the woodpecker, especially around the trunks of the trees.

Where these woods merge into a meadow, look for additional birds in clumps of bushes or small trees. Look high for the waxwing and goldfinch and for an occasional kingbird. Look a little lower for the yellow warbler and the chestnut-sided warbler and for the field sparrow. If it is wintertime, you probably will see a junco close to the ground.

TREE SWALLOW
Iridoprocne bicolor

BOBOLINK
Dolichonyx oryzivorus

MEADOWLARK
Sturnella magna magna

BLUEBIRD
Sialia sialis sialis

GOLDFINCH
Spinus tristis tristis

GOLDEN PLOVER
Pluvialis dominica

In the meadow itself you may see a meadowlark or a bobolink. But you are less certain to see the several sparrows of the field — not because of their scarcity but because of their shyness and concealment. The birds of the shore are quite different. Of these birds, the sandpiper, killdeer, and plover are the ones which are most commonly found there. These are different from the birds whose home is the orchard — especially if the trees still have dead branches where they may make their homes. Here are the house sparrow and the starling, the woodpecker and the flicker circling the tree trunk, the polite little chickadee, the joyous bluebird, the scolding wren, the acrobatic little nuthatch, and the screech owl.

If this appears to be a bonanza of birds, consider the marshland but venture into it only if you are familiar with that kind of terrain. There, you'll find not only the duck in wide variety but possibly also the goose and loon, and maybe a long-legged heron. There are more, too — their species depending upon whether your marshland is in the North or the South.

You'll find as your route takes you from open ground into where the undergrowth is fairly dense, that here, as with the backyard plantings, are open spaces, too. Sunlight warms the birds, dries the wet feathers, and benefits the plants and berry bushes, which feed many of these birds or the insects that some of them eat. These denser bushes and trees furnish protection for the birds from winds, cold, and predators, as do the backyard plantings. In fact, experience in finding birds in your backyard plantings helps you in knowing, almost at a glance, just where you probably will spot birds *here*. Almost certainly you will find an area where birds abound; remember these areas so that you may return to them. When you do return, you probably will be able to spot still more birds. That's because you are learning not only *where* to look for them, but also how nature tries to conceal them by color and design (camouflage) and by their posture against their own kind of background. The bittern, for example, nesting among reeds, will raise its long bill and extend its long neck upward — remaining motionless, and resembling just another reed among the many which surround it.

Since your route may take you also along streams or ponds which attract birds, remember to wear sturdy shoes, preferably boots. These will protect your feet from getting wet and from the underbrush.

The best time of day for bird watching is early morning, when the birds are searching for food after their night's rest. With any luck at all, you'll make an unusual observation, perhaps a bird rarely seen in this part of the country. Recording it and other observations, too, increases both the fun and value of bird watching.

RECORD KEEPING

There is a variety of ways to keep records, but one thing is important to them all, accuracy. Even though you start your records with only a small notebook, keep your entries as accurate as your observations. Promptness in making these entries will increase their accuracy.

Experience will help you to make more complete entries. Some day you may help in the famous Christmas Bird Count. This is an annual census of birds, on one day during Christmas week, taken by groups of bird watchers, who are given territories about fifteen miles in diameter, under the direction of the Audubon Society. Since there are an estimated seven or eight billion birds in America, this census cannot be a counting of each beak. It does provide, though, a *pattern* of where and in what numbers certain species of birds winter. The areas assigned are carefully chosen, for they should be typical of that region of the country. From the information each area yields, a total picture of numbers, species, and concentration can be attempted. All the more reason, then, for the bird watchers, who take this count, to select their routes most carefully. For just as the area itself is representative, so also must the *route* be representative of the area: if the area is two-thirds open country and one-third wooded, the route should be in the same proportion. Also, it is likely the territory consists of only one major vegetative type. A description is given in each "area count report" of these routes, describing their geography and vegetative types. All reports together should then show a typical representation of the terrain of the fifty states.

From these come the counts — samples, really, of the total population of the birds present. Although its participants have fun, even in the cold, dark, early, winter morning the Christmas Bird Count is not a game. It is, on the contrary, a careful census of species and numbers, taken scientifically with camera, binoculars, telescopes, field guides, and a great deal of enthusiasm and pleasure. In 1961, some ten thousand bird watchers, mostly amateurs, hiked or rode through woods, fields, swamps, and hills in all fifty

GREAT BLUE HERON
Ardea herodias herodias

FLICKER
Colaptes auratus luteus

states and, in that one day, reported some fifty million birds of more than five hundred species. But not until these reports were checked and published by the Audubon Field Notes were they accepted as official.

Counting migrating birds at night as they fly past the full harvest moon is another part of bird watching that is sure to start you wondering afresh about this mystery of the birds. Perhaps you will share in the keeping of a Bird Calendar, a record of the return of birds in the spring: *which* species of bird, the date it was first seen *this* season, where, and by whom.

Your records, if you keep them accurately and completely, eventually may have value not only to you but also to others. They may contain information which, by itself or pieced together with another set, can answer one of the many questions still unanswered about the birds. That is why not only your records but your *observing* should be as accurate and as complete as you can learn to do. The more accurate these are, the more rewarding you will find them to be: not just "what is that bird doing?" but the details of the "what." True, that bird is building a nest. But is it the female? Does the male bring building materials? Does the female accept them? (Many don't.) What are

DOWNY WOODPECKER
Dryobates pubeseens medianus

SPOTTED SANDPIPER
Actitis macularia

these? Did the male build a nest, during courting, which the female now ignores? Do *both* birds work to build the nest? *How* is it built — and how supported? The more you observe, the more you learn. It works in the opposite way, too: the more you learn, the more you can observe — and can enjoy.

You may discover that you'd like to keep records not just of counts or by seasons but, rather, to make a life study of some feature of bird life in which you have become especially interested. Here again the local chapter of the Audubon Society or of the other groups, listed in the back of this book, can help you in organizing and following this study.

Such organizations as these sometimes sponsor an original article, if it has scientific value, written by one who has observed carefully and discovered something about bird life which was little known before. These societies welcome not only the skilled bird watcher but the beginner, too. He is invited into this company of bird watchers more experienced than he — people ready to share their knowledge with him and to help him enjoy his hobby to the fullest.

BIRD CLUBS: If you don't know the name and address of the bird club nearest you, write the National Audubon Society, 1130 Fifth Avenue, New York, N.Y. 10028. This Society also has its own junior bird watcher organization, the Audubon Junior Club.

The National Audubon Society also can supply very inexpensively the following:

    Bird Picture Cards
    Daily Field Card of Bird
    Birdlife Card
    Bird File

The Society also has checklists and life lists of birds to be found in your section of the country; and pamphlets of local bird life (which you may also be able to secure from your State Department of Agriculture or Conservation). The Fish and Wildlife Service of the U.S. Department of the Interior, Washington 25, D.C. can provide information:

    Locations of wildlife refuges (for field trips)
    Conservation Bulletins
        Attracting Birds (Conservation Bulletin #1)
        Plantings (Conservation Bulletin #7)
        Food for Birds (Conservation Bulletin #14)
        Others of specialized interest.

Your State Fish and Game Commission can give you information and possibly assistance in coping with squirrels and other pests to birds.

FEEDING: Information taken from *Conservation Bulletin #1,* Fish & Wildlife Service, U.S. Department of the Interior, *Attracting Birds* by W. L. McAtee. For sale by the Superintendent of Documents, U.S. Government Printing Office, Washington, D.C. 20025.

Woodpeckers	Suet, corn, cracked nuts
Jays	Suet, corn, cracked nuts, peanuts, sunflower seeds
Titmice, chickadees, nuthatches	Suet, shelled and broken peanuts, cracked nuts, sunflower seeds, bread crumbs
Mockingbirds, catbirds, robins, thrashers, hermit thrushes	Cut apples and oranges, raisins, currants bread crumbs
Starlings	Cut apples, raisins, currants, suet, scratch feed, scraps from the table
Blackbirds, cardinals, towhees	Sunflower seeds, corn, scratch feed, shelled or broken peanuts
Juncos, finches, sparrows	Scratch feed, wheat, millet, small seed mixtures, bread crumbs

These foods also include the following kinds: fat other than suet, pork rinds, bones with some shreds of meat, cured cheese, buckwheat, crackers, crumbs, coconut meat, corn bread, cornmeal, dog biscuits, stale doughnuts, piecrust, dried fruits, and hominy. Soft moist foods are acceptable except in weather so cold that they freeze. Avoid salty foods.

PLANTINGS: In *Conservation Bulletin #17,* Fish & Wildlife Service, U.S. Department of the Interior, W. L. McAtee lists the many fleshy fruits and the popularity of each among birds, as well as those birds known to eat each kind. In summary, he lists these in *Conservation Bulletin #1* in the order of their popularity with birds: raspberry, blackberry and elderberry; juniper and red cedar genus, bayberry, mulberry, pokeberry, strawberry, sumac, grape, dogwood, and blueberry; greenbrier, hackberry, crab and flowering apple genus, juneberry, thorn apple, rose, crowberry, holly, Virginia creeper, sour gum, bearberry and manzanita genus, huckleberry, snowberry, and viburnum (blackhaw, cranberrybush, and others).

As an example of what may be found in *Conservation Bulletin #17,* the desirable kinds of birds known to eat the raspberry and blackberry are listed as: ruffed and sharp-tailed grouse, bob-white, Eastern flicker, red-headed woodpecker, Eastern kingbird, tufted titmouse, wren tit, mockingbird, catbird, brown thrasher, robin, wood and Swainson's thrushes, Eastern bluebird, cedar waxwing, red-eyed vireo, orchard and Baltimore orioles, cardinal, rose-breasted, black-headed, and pine grosbeaks, Eastern, spotted and brown towhees, white-throated, fox, and song sparrows.

Blueberry eaters are listed there as: ruffed grouse, greater prairie chicken, sharp-tailed grouse, bob-white, California quail, wild turkey, Eastern kingbird, black-capped chickadee, tufted titmouse, catbird, brown thrasher, robin, hermit thrush, Eastern bluebird, cedar waxwing, orchard oriole, cardinal, pine grosbeak, Eastern towhee, and tree sparrow.

WILDLIFE LEAFLET #223, *National Plantings for Attracting Waterfowl to Marsh and Other Water Areas,* is also from the Fish & Wildlife Service. To augment the supply of food and cover for waterfowl, it recommends such plants as muskgrasses, wigeongrass, sago pondweed, wild celery, etc. It also tells how to plant those given in that publication, and lists dealers in duck-food plants.

Plants which attract hummingbirds are those whose flowers are red, preferably, or orange or purple: day lilies, lilies, cannas, bouncing bet, spiderflower, red buckeye, morning glories, petunias and others. Dealers in bird-attracting devices sell a glass feeder which, when filled with one part sugar and two part's water, is said to attract these tiny, hovering birds.

Plants which feed seedeaters (the sparrow group, juncos, goldfinches and the like) are: prince's-feather, love-lies-bleeding, blessed thistle, rock purslanes, centaureas, cosmos, forget-me-nots, prince's-plume, portulaca, and others. Trees which yield food for seedeaters are listed as: alders, birches, ashes, box elders, elms, larches, pines, oaks and beechs.

Your state agricultural department probably can inform you which plantings are best able to survive in *your* locale. Also, you will find an extraordinarily good set of information on plantings in *Songbirds in Your Garden* by John K. Terres, who suggests not only what is good for the birds but also what is desirable for you.

THE SCIENCE-HOBBY SERIES
Science-Hobby Book of Archaeology
Science-Hobby Book of Aquariums
Science-Hobby Book of Bird Watching
Science-Hobby Book of Boating
Science-Hobby Book of Fishing
Science-Hobby Book of Rocks and Minerals
Science-Hobby Book of Shell Collecting
Science-Hobby Book of Terrariums
Science-Hobby Book of Weather Forecasting

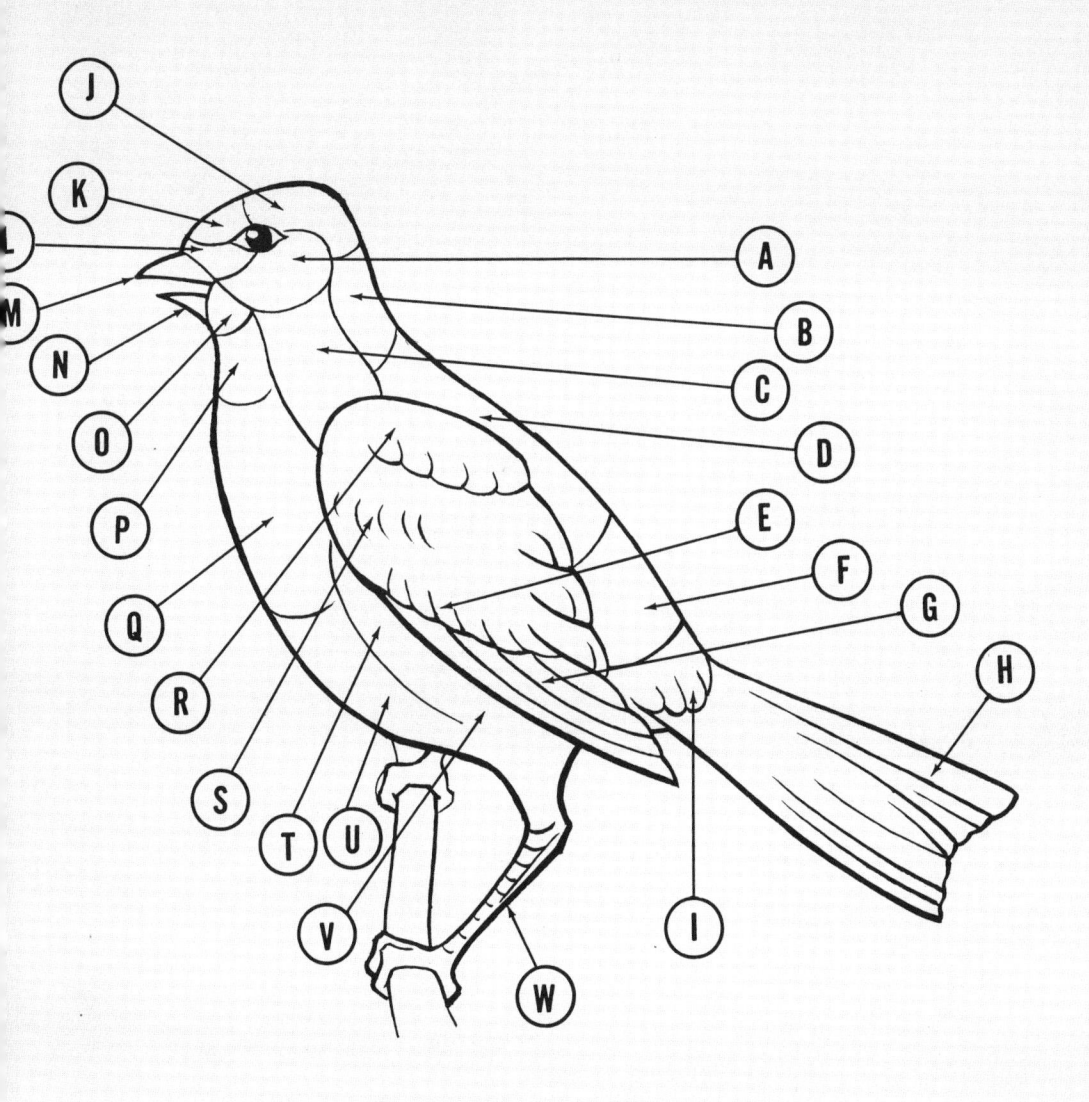

TOPOGRAPHY OF A BIRD

A. CHEEK
B. NAPE
C. SIDE OF NECK
D. BACK
E. SECONDARIES
F. RUMP
G. PRIMARIES
H. OUTER TAIL FEATHERS
I. UPPER TAIL COVERTS
J. CROWN
K. FOREHEAD
L. LORE

M. UPPER MANDIBLE
N. LOWER MANDIBLE
O. CHIN
P. THROAT
Q. BREAST
R. SHOULDER
S. WING BARS
T. SIDE
U. BELLY
V. FLANK
W. TARSUS

We specialize in publishing quality books for
young people. For a complete list please write
Lerner Publications Company
241 First Avenue North, Minneapolis, Minnesota 55401

CASS CO. R-VIII ELEMENTARY SCHOOLS
GARDEN CITY URICH, MISSOURI